Odd Evening

Odd Evening

Eric McHenry

WAYWISER

First published in 2016 by

THE WAYWISER PRESS

Christmas Cottage, Church Enstone, Chipping Norton, Oxon OX7 4NN, UK
P.O. Box 6205, Baltimore, MD 21206, USA
http://waywiser-press.com

Editor-in-Chief
Philip Hoy

Senior American Editor
Joseph Harrison

Associate Editors
Dora Malech | Eric McHenry | V. Penelope Pelizzon | Clive Watkins
Greg Williamson | Matthew Yorke

A CIP catalogue record for this book is available from the British Library

ISBN 978-1-904130-68-0

Printed and bound by
T. J. International Ltd., Padstow, Cornwall, PL28 8RW

for my family

Acknowledgments

I owe so much to so many – the most to my wife and children, my parents and brother, and my grandparents. This book owes itself to the Topeka poets, the Seattle poets, and the Boston poets. Boundless gratitude to Washburn University for a Sweet Sabbatical, the Sewanee Writers' Conference for a fellowship, Nicholas Garland and Priscilla Roth for London and Chedworth, and Kelly Magerkurth for the exquisite photographs. And many thanks to the editors of the following magazines and journals for publishing my poems:

Able Muse: "The Drift," "how can i," "Odd Evening" "One Good Shove," "Randy Used the Word"
Cincinnati Review: "Found Poem"
Common Knowledge: "EGOT," "Joke," "Looking Up," "Summer Mix," "Turkeys and Strippers"
Field: "You're Back"
Flint Hills Review: "Street View"
Poetry International: "16 Suite" (section 1 and the first stanza of section 4), "At the Baptist Mission," "Copying the Master," "Crying With Glasses On," "Ether Monument," "First Responder"
Poetry Northwest: "Add Dylan Klebold as a Friend," "Deathbed Confession," "New Year's Letter to All the Friends I've Estranged by Not Writing," "The Space," "Stay," "Unfinished Attic"
Queen Mob's Tea House: "Cicadas"
Salamander: "Assisted Living," "The Darker Grass," "Five-Legged Spider," "The Song of Stationary Nathan"
Seattle Review: "16 Suite" (section 2, as "The Worst"), "Apparent," "Transaction"
Slate: "How to Steal the Laptop of Your Childhood Nemesis"
Terrain.org: "The Pass-Through"
Topeka Magazine: "The Gil Carter Correspondence," "The Last Payphone in Topeka"
Yale Review: "Canes"

"Add Dylan Klebold as a Friend," "Deathbed Confession," and

"Stay" received the 2010 Theodore Roethke Prize from *Poetry Northwest*. "Apparent" was reprinted in *Many Trails to the Summit* (Rose Alley Press) and in *The Journal*. "Looking Up" and "Summer Mix" were reprinted on *Poetry Daily*. "New Year's Letter to All the Friends I've Estranged by Not Writing" was reprinted by Pentameter Press as part of the Poetry by Post broadside series. "16 Suite" (Section 2) was reprinted by *The Stranger* as part of the Seattle Poetry Chain series. "Transaction" was reprinted in *seveneightfive*.

CONTENTS

1. Five-Legged Spider

2. You're Back

3. Odd Evening

CONTENTS

1. Five-Legged Spider

Found Poem

They're coming like a thunderhead.
They're darkening the eastern plain.
All afternoon we've watched them spread
across it like a pinot stain.

They're coming in marsupial fur
with dull teeth and confusing hair.
They're coming out of Flumminster
to prove that they can come from there.

They crave our license and detest
our license plate. That much is known.
They misidentify our crest
as a corruption of their own.

They're coming for the final word.
They'll enter by a guardless gate.
Their footfall was the first we'd heard
of their approach, and it's too late

to bribe our common god, or buy
a better omen from the auspex,
too late to flee or fortify
a city built for pleasant prospects.

They're coming for us. Like tomorrow,
they'll enter by the eastern gate.
They've got their history of sorrow.
They want us to participate.

New Year's Letter to All the Friends I've Estranged
by Not Writing

I'm sorry, first of all,
for the impersonal
medium. It's midnight and I'm spread
so thin I just about said spin so thread.
Sage came home with a strip of masking tape
across her lunchbox: PLEASE SLICE EVERY GRAPE.
And there again I've put a blameless child
between us like a human shield
against accountability, and then
acknowledged it. And there again.
As though by self-embarrassment alone
I might regress
into a truer self, becoming small
and solid as the last matryoshka doll;
as though that might redress
the failings up to which I've failed to own:
that I've identified too closely with
myself, or with my sympathetic myth;
I've acted as though it were all an act —
the first of five; I've called the fact
the brutal fact and failed to call
the fourth wall down a *wall*.
And all while waiting for the world to drop
me, you, and Jody at a common stop
so you could keep me company again,
which would require the world to be a train.
The world's a wheel. The world's a rolling pin.
The world is spinning thread and spreading thin.
I can't imagine what this goes to prove
except the obvious — I'd rather move
than mow. But you asked whether the address
you have for me is current: No. Yes.

Unfinished Attic

Good for you if you still want to know
what words your mouth will make when you implore
God or a shoeless murderer to show
himself or mercy — I don't anymore.
Scanning a row of plastic tubs, I swore
I saw a human foot, and when one toe
moved and sent motion through the other four
I started saying *whoa whoa whoa whoa whoa*.
I didn't drop what I was holding, though:
a box of candle stubs I'd come to store
with all the other gauds we lived below —
paint cans with painted lips, spray cans of snow,
gilt paper clinging to its cardboard core,
mirrors (the foot was mine) and *whoa whoa whoa*.

16 Suite

1.

Because I only kissed her
because she looked like you,
I didn't blame your sister
for spitting in my drink
at Pizza Hut. (She tried
to stir it in, but it
was clear, coherent spit
and wasn't going to sink.)
All spring and summer I'd
avoided her because
I was so sure she knew.
Then one day there I was,
expecting her to bring
me breadsticks on a tray,
and Pepsi, and to say
How was everything?

2.

No, the worst was watching Darren trip
comically on his own hightop, pitch
facelong into a concrete wheelstop, chip
his tooth and split his chin. "It's just a bitch,"

Troy said. For fifteen minutes Darren lay
there in a parking space, spat blood, and slid
his tongue through the black gap we didn't say
made him look stupider although it did.

How grateful for that one astringent truth,
how stunned by its sufficiency, we were.
Darren, you are going to wear that tooth
to school and that's a bitch and that's for sure.

3.

Interest in your face began to flag
when you got contacts. Pretty soon the kid
who thought it was hilarious to tag
buildings with your name no longer did.

Walking out of People's with a pail,
a steel brush and a five-pound bag of lye,
you were the kind of person words would fail,
in just a few more hours, to signify.

4.

You didn't find the sugar maples' turning
all that dramatic, and you didn't find
the purple 37 in the square
of pastel dots because it wasn't there.
You may have chosen not to finish learning
you were profoundly red-green colorblind
until you were 16 and didn't care,
because by then believing wasn't seeing
and every non-experience was true
to your experience of experience being
available to everyone but you.

But you experienced those leaves, those days,
as atmosphere. You raked them into piles
and to the cul de sac to supervise,
and watched the cinders climb into the haze
that overhung the city's four square miles,
and that was how they finally met your eyes,
and now, and years from now, the tang and sting
of maple leafsmoke on November air,
or in your clothes, or in the clothes or hair
of someone passing will retrieve a pang
so imprecise it's briefly everything.

The Space

After a decade of incontinence
he looked at cantaloupe and it went bad,
moved only for the girl who changed his pad,
lost sixty pounds and died in self-defense,
then for a minute lay there making sense
while we defied him — Uncle Doug and Dad
discussed the father they no longer had
in indoor voices and the present tense.
I found his still-expiring plastic mask
oppressive, but was glad to have a task,
and when I slid my thumb between its band
and his cool head I thought of the still-warm
space between his ribs and upper arm,
and found it, briefly, with my other hand.

Assisted Living

Because she isn't fast
enough, most days, to rouse
the plastic Santa Claus
who shakes his hips and calls
on us to deck these halls
each time I push her past
his cotton-smothered shelf,
she likes to wheel herself.

The Last Payphone in Topeka

The passing stranger used to jingle.
Now he has no use for change.
His ringtone is a CeeLo single
and you're the one who's passing strange.

When I approach you on your corner
or in your stuffy entryway,
I'll do it mutely, like a mourner.
Respects are all I've come to pay.

Payphone, I hope your standing slumber
feels like a belly full of dimes
and sings you endless local-number
sequences like nursery rhymes:

266-9637.
232-4829.
354-9027.
And 233-5101,

which was my grandmother until
she moved herself to Brewster Place.
The odd tetrameter can still
summon a voice but not a face.

Payphone, I know the elegy
is just another obsolete
technology technology
has stranded on another street,

but so is everything worthwhile:
grandmothers, moonshots, shards of clay,
the square of squares we tried to dial,
the only tone that won't decay.

Ether Monument

Because he can't drink at the supper, Shane,
whose habits are the pain they palliate,
is trying not to drop a paper plate
of ravioli, garlic bread, and rain.

Because he can't drink at the shelter either,
tonight he plans to lay his burden
down like a bedroll in the Public Garden
beside a fountain *to commemorate*

that the inhaling of ether
causes insensibility to pain.

Deathbed Confession

"In 1971 a man calling himself Dan Cooper hijacked a plane from Portland to Seattle, demanded parachutes and $200,000 in cash, then jumped into the night with the money, never to be seen again." — fbi.gov

So little seemed to be at stake.
The bomb was real; the threat was fake.
Neither was difficult to make.

And I was in my element,
or nearly there. Yes, the descent
was cold, but warmer as I went,

and yes it was coal-black and raining,
but I had uppers and my training.
I've spent my whole life not complaining.

When I could see the woods I wandered
out with the twenties, which I laundered,
safety-deposited, and squandered,

and with the oddest thing, a name
I'd paid for but could never claim,
a private joke, my private fame.

That's been the hardest part: denial —
remaining of no interest while
the Bureau opened up a file

on every former paratrooper
who in his final morphine stupor
discovered he was D.B. Cooper.

I'm D.B. Cooper. There, I said it.
It's decent work if you can get it,
but it pays cash. There is no credit,

or blame, or pity in thin air,
and I've spent forty winters there.
I'll take whatever you can spare,

although I don't suppose the guy
whose last confession was a lie
deserves it any less than I.

First Responder

The streetlamps think it's still last night.
Is it too early to disturb
the guy who's mostly on the curb?
He's probably just passed out, right?

He isn't so much prone as fetal.
The sheer unnatural whiteness of
his hand is probably a glove.
The air is bracing but not fatal.

And I can't see his face, of course.
He may be looking for the source
of something his Tercel is leaking —
very, very intently looking.

The second thing they'll want to know
is if I've found him unresponsive,
and when they find me unresponsive
they'll take that as a yes and no.

EGOT

"That stands for Emmy, Grammy, Oscar and Tony, the awards [Philip Michael Thomas] has set out to win. ... He wears a gold medallion emblazoned with the letters." — Trish Janeshutz and Rob MacGregor, *The Making of Miami Vice*

Philip Michael went to Cali,
dropped the Dino with the valet,
pulled the gold from his Armani:
Emmy, Grammy, Oscar, Tony.

Rico rolled into Miami
seeking justice, sand and Sonny,
found some clothes that fit the weather:
Eenie, Meanie, Miney, Money.

Rico rolled into Miami,
found the dude who'd killed his brother,
knocked him over with a feather,
tucked the gold pulled out the jammy:

Oscar, Tony, Emmy, Grammy —
none of these according to my
source; of course it also spells
his name with one too many *l*s.

Philip Michael Thomas went to
Cali riding in a Pinto,
something, something, macaroni:
Emmy, Grammy, Oscar, Tony.

You know how this movie ends —
sketchy neighbors, psychic friends,
Disney's *Positively Minnie,*
table scraps of daytime dramas.

You say Philip Michael Thomas
never did fulfill his promise.

27

History may say he carries
episodes if not the series.

Hunger, Anger, Honor, Ennui,
Philip, when we said dream on we
meant it both ways — that's not funny.
Eenie, Meanie, Miney, Money.

Five-Legged Spider

for a girl who lost her father

She's heard of sadness but not anguish.
Her uncle thinks we ought to gather
stories now for when she's older
and trying to distinguish
memories from what we've told her.

I'm trying to explain her father
to my impassive camera-phone
but finding I don't have the strength
to hold it steady at arm's length
for half a minute, let alone

to look it in the pinhole eye
and summon every memory
he'd want to be remembered by
and put three sentences together
that don't sound summary.

Come down to me, five-legged spider.
Come take a spacewalk through
the orbit of my stuffy head
on one sheer, super-tensile thread
and complicate my view.

Come down and ask me to consider
the heroism of my hand,
which, like you, doesn't understand
asymmetry but knows
precisely when to self-oppose.

I'm confident I can't diminish
you further in a parable
I can't finish.
Show me the strange, arrhythmic strider
whose body is still bearable.

2. You're Back

You're Back

1.

You went away and they went on
without you. When you reappeared
with kids and an ironic beard
the ticket carousel was full.
They'd finally stopped taking orders
from east of Dougal and redrawn
the map's eccentric ballpoint borders.
The dough hook dervished in its bowl.

Home is where your references
aren't recognized, or needed — when you
have to go back they have to clock you in.
The only other differences
were little changes to the menu.
Nobody asked you where you'd been.

2.

Your daughter didn't have a single friend
named Stephanie, in soccer or at school.
Nobody screamed the name at either end
of the public pool.

And you began to understand, and mourn,
that there would have to be a great-grandmother
named Stephanie before there could be another
Stephanie born.

And the three Stephanies who gave the name
its amplitude, the Stephanies of myth,
kept showing up at Kroger and became
the Stephanies you went to high school with.

3.

You went away and they went on
like that, as though you hadn't gone,
still doing it the way they'd learned
to do it and that only they
still do it and the only way
as far as they're concerned.
Then you came back and said I knew it
and told them you were unaware
of anybody anywhere
still doing it the way they do it,
and they said you don't say.

You're Back

4.

Only your first-grade teacher looked the same —
uncannily, because it was her daughter.
She had the makeup and had kept the name.
She even had the belly you could rub
for good luck when she brought you in to sub.
And she had plans to finish out the year,
but you'd been through this once before; her water
would break in April and she'd disappear
for thirty years and you'd be back like Kotter,
back to the blackboard, suddenly unsure
of how best to distinguish *your* from *you're*:
You're back, and bigger; better watch your back —
don't strain it sipping from those tiny fountains.
You're sad because your blackboard isn't black.
You're teaching them your harmlessly subversive
verse/choruses to "Cielito Lindo"
and other lovely, useless things, like cursive.
You're staring out your modular's one window,
turning the thunderheads to thundermountains.

36

The Darker Grass

You hate the easy things to hate:
new buildings and the weird materials
they're made from (gypcrete, carbon fiber, foam),
5-Hour Energy, four-dollar gas,
the newness of the sacrificial grass
in medians, the new arterials
that in another month will narrow
to two lanes so that crews can widen them
to six lanes so that you won't have to wait
your turn to wait your turn for a turn arrow.
You'll drive an extra mile to do your driving
through parts of town that pose no threat of thriving,
which means you've started seeing more
of your old neighborhood, which makes you wonder
if architects are ever paid to render
houses in hypothetical decline,
because that might have helped prepare you for
the seeding lawn, the 6 that's now a 9,
the deposed mini-dish, the single shutter,
the notice Scotch-taped to the door,
the doorless frame, the deviating gutter,
the misaligned and multicolored shingles,
the spraypaint flourishes, the altered angles
of everything including your old block
and your old house, which now looks like a stock
photo from an *Economist* article
on houses that are worth less than the cost
of razing them. If there's a troubled ghost
that haunts that groaning storybook, it's you.
How many midnights have you drifted through
its seven rooms? How long do you intend
to keep your vigil at that particle-
board windowpane before you apprehend
the lost colonial across the street,
the one that overlooked the neighborhood

paternally and got out while it could,
its front walk still advancing through the grass
in concrete increments to meet
the darker grass where the foundation was?

Joke

Guy walks into a bar, says what do you recommend.
Bartender says I've got bitters, cocktail onions and fizz.
The jukebox plays only national anthems
and the dartboard can experience pain.
Guy says I'm not sure I'm comfortable
with that. Bartender says make yourself comfortable.

Turkeys and Strippers

whose breasts have swollen into such fantastic butterballs
they'd pull you earthward if you weren't immobile in your stalls,

beagles with nicotine addictions, sheep with human faces,
you, with your orthodontic headgear snagged on your leg braces,

who apprehend that only half the litter will survive,
and they by eating, slowly, even littler things alive,

you who subsistence-fished a river dammed for hydropower
to keep a mayor ruddy in his hydra-headed shower,

you who were offered clemency for silence and chose right,
then left town without going home to get your clothes, Mose Wright,

you who saw the demand for bodies driving the supply,
you to whose bodies any of the following apply:

that won't quit, permanently like that, disappeared, displayed,
ungovernable, of which an example has been made,

orphans of lynching bee and Little Boy and Littleton,
Bataan, baton, Tonton Macoute, and 50-megaton

roadside, pipe, fire, thermonuclear, and cherry bomb,
torturers put to torture, Jeffrey Dahmer, Jerry, Tom,

antagonists who saw yourselves conveniently maimed
or heard your common suffering creatively renamed —

wig-splitting, wisdom-acquisition, wetting, necklacing —
and you who lived through Operation Not One Living Thing,

please raise your phantom hand and take the Phantom Oath with me:
When I have power I am going to use it differently.

Add Dylan Klebold as a Friend

(2009)

dude did you hear
the spirit squad
like pimped the doubletree

for our 10 year
reunion god
how tragic will that be

i thought about
you in 01
and what you would of said

when they came out
with halo 1
we all knew doom was dead

dude what the fuck
is up with yr
profile pic oh well

i guess were stuck
with who we were
in high school lol

Canes

We should entrust them only to the old.
A cane suggests authority or sport
to anyone who doesn't need support.
A prefect who discovers he can hold
one by the shaft, or even upside-down,
will feel the verb vibrating in the noun.

A prefect is a boy. However deft
his mouth becomes at publicly explaining
the rector's protocol for public caning,
his hand is more accustomed to the heft
and balance of a cricket bat, and trembles
to grip a cane like what it half-resembles.

A prefect may impulsively suspend
your sentence after six or seven blows
when he hears titters from the first few rows,
re-grip the cane by its unhandled end,
wait for the tremor traveling through the room
to clench into attention, and resume.

A lifetime of reliving this may leave
you oversatisfied with your own fitness
to judge events you did and didn't witness
and unreceptive when you first receive
a crabbed apology for an unnamed
"sad incident of which I'm still ashamed."

Push up your reading glasses and allow
bemusement to resolve, first into rage
at the translucent, single-sided page,
the fantasy that there must be, somehow,
fraternity in your respective traumas,
his near-demotion, your blood-stiff pyjamas,

then into a desire to disabuse,
then into wondering about that word,
then into bed, where you may rest assured
that any cane you dream you can refuse,
re-grip, or even raise, because your hand
is steady and you need no help to stand.

You'll wake up feeling generous and glib
and answer him at length without rereading
his letter, and you'll leave no letter bleeding,
applying steady pressure to the nib,
producing but not pausing to admire
the measured strokes such sentences require.

Copying the Master

Your book falls open to reveal
the poems I wish were mine
because those were the leaves I spread
widest on the scanner bed,
leaning with the heel
of my right hand until I heard the spine.

At the Baptist Mission

In your translation you relieved the Bible
of its possessive case, because you knew
that ownership had no place in the tribal
vernacular, although that isn't true.

It's true that they relieved you of your tense,
and maybe one possessive, when you died.
They didn't like significant events
estranging names from what they signified.

According to the 1820 census,
no one was here. A bison understands
the need for new translations, because sense is
a property and properties change hands.

According to one of the seventeen
surviving speakers, you were fair and good.
She said your honorary name might mean
Prayed Slowly or *Believed He Understood*.

Transaction

I say loiter, you say hang: loiter.
Sir, do we look like a gang to you?
That officer said we look like a gang.
We must look like a gang. He said we do.

She's black, about 16. Her clothes are blue.
Her friends are black. Their clothes are blue and red.
The Jayhawks are at home tonight; KU
clings like a snowcap to Mt. Oread.

Sir, do we look like a gang to you?
My friends and I? She's livid and polite.
It's Friday night. Their clothes are red and blue.
They're out on Mass. because it's Friday night.

They're out on Massachusetts Street, named for
the home state of the man who gave the land
beneath it and of whose deeds any more
history might force the poem's hand.

Thank you, she says. But what else can she say?
It isn't satisfaction on her face.
Of *course*, I tell her, and I'm on my way
uphill again, a credit to my race.

Randy Used the Word

When Randy used the word as though
it were a word that anyone might use,
I don't know what I thought. I flared his cape
with my forearms and shifted in his chair.
I know I didn't think of Tony's hair,
a hi-top fade that Randy would have no
idea how to fix. I know I said
nothing, by which I must have meant *Continue
filling my ears with trimmings. Dust my nape
with talcum. Offer me impartial views
of both sides of the back of my head.*

*And outside, let the barber's pole continue
its reenactment. Let the silver ball recall
the bowl of leeches. Let the helical
progress-illusion of the stripes remain
the blood, the twining bandage, and the vein.*

America, and I'm about to talk
directly to the Eric in you,
you had to pay for that one, but
the man you say you mean to be will walk
out of some barbershops with his hair half-cut.

The Pass-Through

I voice that terminal *r* when I say
Dang brother was you thirsty?
because I know I want to be black the way
I want to be an architect or gay.
My longings are sincere and touristy.

Your job, remember, is to slide the tray
we've loaded with everybody's empty glasses
onto the belt whose job is to convey
it past the black man whose job is to say
Dang brother was you thirsty? as it passes.

Because I need one, my job is to tell
the story but not too well.
So, for example, I leave out the wall,
the pass-through, and the black hands that were all
you and he would ever see of each other.

I leave out every window that obscures
what it reveals: I leave out sickle-cell,
your passing, and the ground that I've allowed
to come between us — everything but *brother*.
I press my freckled nose to its frosted glass.

Sometimes when I think the story aloud
I catch myself relaxing the *r*s
and flattering my voice that it could pass.

Stay

(Frost)

Fall's first gold is green.
It falls somewhere between
a joy and a concern.
But soon the leaves will turn
flamboyant with their doubt,
like people falling out
of love, becoming all
the lovelier as they fall.

3. Odd Evening

how can i

how can i keep from singing is the thing
autocomplete assumes you want to know.
Release your next breath noisily, as though
announcing your decision not to sing.
Think of your body as a cello string
distraction might pass over like a bow.
Think of Topeka as a Broadway show
that only you can keep from opening.
Be glad that you're not genuinely eager
to keep from singing; then you'd hit return,
elated to have found yourself, and learn
about the folk song lifted by Pete Seeger
from the back pocket of a Baptist pew
that everyone's been searching for but you.

The Song of Stationary Nathan

(Yeats)

I went out to the maple tree
because a riot was in its head,
and flung a Frisbee at the noise,
but brought a starling down instead,
and laid it in a shoebox nest,
and put some twigs and Skittles in,
and struggled up, and set it back
where I imagined it had been.

As I was shinnying down, I felt
a Skittle windfall on my head.
A skinny girl in red capris
was pelting me with green and red.
She swung her legs and laughed my name,
then disappeared into the crown.
I followed her until the swaying
and broken sunlight brought me down.

Though I am old with waiting here,
and she has grown up and away,
I'll watch the tossing of those boughs
and catch her silhouette someday,
and we'll walk lightly up the boughs,
and gather, in eternal June,
the Nilla Wafers of the sun,
the Necco Wafers of the moon.

Cicadas

"Are Topeka dreams the lullaby of lurve?"

1.

A portmanteau of learning curve.
Hit me with your best downvotes.
I've been eleven and in lurve
and I know what the word denotes.

The way a larva spells its name,
knowing the preferred nomenclature
is *nymph*. Cicadas have no shame.
Thanks, nature,

for the new neighbors whose lives are porn,
drone metal and unlicensed flying.
Mine would be too if I'd been born
seventeen and dying.

The maples were so loud this year
my daughter had to sit up streaming
Netflix because she couldn't hear
herself dreaming.

2.

Lullabier, lullabier,
univocal as a choir,
tell me this about the bough:
if you do or don't allow
that its object is to break,
how long will it wait to make
you a prophet or a liar,
lullabier, lullabier?

Odd Evening

I didn't know you were a twin
until I saw you dancing through
a doorway you were standing in.
I didn't know you were a twin,
and if, since then, I haven't been
myself with you, it isn't you.
I didn't know you were a twin
until I saw you dancing through.

How to Steal the Laptop of Your Childhood Nemesis

She keeps a spare key in a hollow rock
outside the kitchen door she doesn't lock.
Her lights are on. Her sheltie is all talk.
You shouldn't need the code for the alarm
(1234) because she tried to arm
the thermostat again. You're getting warm.
Her master suite smells like a Hallmark store.
Her vanity is huge. Try to ignore
the fact that everything's a metaphor
and that I've let you walk right into it.
Blow out the Yankee Candles she left lit.
Take in the master bathroom. Take a shit.
Flush resolutely. Agitate the handle.
Refill the Softsoap. Light a Yankee Candle.
Her MacBook Pro is hiding, like the Grail,
in plain sight; anyone but you will fail
to realize it's not a bathroom scale.
Open her desktop. Close her Yahoo! Mail.
She keeps her recent photos in a folder
called "Photos." Click a thumbnail and behold her
in sunlight, in a champagne off-the-shoulder
sheath wedding dress, fussed over by attendants.
She's forty and has come into resplendence
like an inheritance, like heirloom pendants
flattering ear and flawless collarbone.
I should have told you, or you should have known,
that she has changed the most and aged the least
of all your enemies, her face uncreased
by laughter, worry, shame, or self-denial.
Those are her cheekbones. That's her cryptic smile.
Those are her footsteps on the kitchen tile.

Crying With Glasses On

It's such a grownup thing to do.
Like renting tap shoes to perform
for no one in an electrical storm.
What's wrong with you?

Remove your spectacles and cry,
already. If there's rain
on your side of the windowpane
you're probably the sky.

What's the intention of a tear
if not to lubricate and cleanse?
I'll tell you: a corrective lens
is making things too clear.

In college I could see the future
coming and would often
pop out my contacts first, to soften
its least attractive feature.

If you'll just give it half an hour,
grief will discover
you drawing steam-roses in the shower,
and join you, like a lover.

Summer Mix

For seven dog years, Uncle Mark, I've meant
to say my god that summer mix you sent
is awesome. Every song's a winner on it.
Telephone Road should not exist. I mean
how can a sound so cluttered sound so clean
I could eat Brian Wilson's dinner on it?

How can one note so clarify another,
brother once-removed? I love my mother
and father and some Simon & Garfunkel
records but, off the record, who are they?
Novelists say context, painters say
perspective and the rest of us say uncle.

I'm on the level part of the back lawn
with Richard Wilbur, but your mix is on,
and his collected magisteria
are going to be closing for the day.
It's mostly homely here. The house is slab,
cinder, and cedar. Some of the grass is crab.
The runner that's about to grab
the downspout is, I think, wisteria,

so that worked out. And Dylan is a faint
buzz from the bedroom Sonja's trying to paint.
But she'll be opening a window soon,
and when she does, because this is an essay,
it will become the mouth that sings his messy
Dignity to the afternoon.

Looking Up

Given a moment, Gavin can explain
why he keeps looking up: because no plane
is coming. Then, because there's no Plan B
to shift to, he'll be shifting to one knee.

The words for which the sky is at a loss
will find themselves, tomorrow, draped across
the roof of some disinterested Cape Cod,
as though they were a message meant for God

alone. They weren't, of course, and you know Gavin
well enough to know what he would've given
to see that sign arrive, to see you see
it sailing into legibility.

That's why, before you say a word, you've got
to let him walk you through the whole foiled plot
and look as though you can't believe he'd try
to pull I LOVE YOU BETH across the sky.

The Gil Carter Correspondence

On the night of August 11, 1959, a minor-league baseball player named Gil Carter hit what is believed to be the longest home run in history, approximately 730 feet. When the ball disappeared over the 60-foot light pole behind the left-field fence, it was still on its way up.

Before he takes his insulin, the man
who hit the really long home run responds
in longhand to another patient fan:
"Thank you so much for writing, Mr. Bonds.

Yes, I remember almost everything,
the nighthawk silhouettes, the infield chatter,
the ball becoming huge, the hitchless swing,
the lone voice swallowing its last *no batter,*

slack faces lifted to the firmament —
and by *the ball* I hope you know I mean
the one that hadn't finished its ascent
the last time it was seen,

which isn't necessarily the one
beside me as I write. It wasn't hard
in '59 to find a fresh home run
in any big New Mexican backyard.

Home run: what a spectacular misnomer.
You can't go home again, jiggity-jog.
If forced to choose a name I'd favor *Homer*,
less for Odysseus than for his dog.

What can I truly say about this ball?
It's horsehide, twine, and yarn from Costa Rica
hugging a hunk of cork from Portugal.
On its slow odyssey to East Topeka

my homer would've been the shortest leg.
I saw the seams that night, the sutured leather,
and realized this was the only egg
horses and men would ever put together,

and that I should reopen it, should try
to beat it back into the cosmic batter
from which we're conjured. Chickens long to fly,
but if an egg can long it longs to shatter.

Of course I couldn't do it. Once again
I took the full cut and it simply flew.
I'd love to tell you how that felt, but then
I wouldn't be the only one who knew."

The Drift

1.

You've seen the fathers carrying away
the fecal sacs like soft pearls in their beaks;
a common grackle fledges in three weeks
but shits the nest a hundred times a day.

They drop them in your pool, because like you
they've come with vague instructions to deliver
their troubles to the purifying river
its waters are a clear allusion to.

2.

You saw the vinyl walls begin to mottle
and gather like a great-grandmother's skin,
and realized your loss, by now, was total
whether you kept it up or filled it in,

and so you stood your ground beside the placid
blue oval that believed it was a pond,
broadcasting shock and cyanuric acid
and humming while your hair went slowly blond.

One Good Shove

Deploy the tilt Sunbrella,
sit down with your ice water,
canned citronella
candles and horseflyswatter,

and watch Aurora huddle
with Snow White, Cinderella,
one newer, darker model
and your daughter.

Sun through the hackberry dapples
the penicillin-pinks
of their overinflated raft.
They've touched no spindles,

bitten no bad apples —
she obviously thinks
they can ride out the summer
on that dubious craft.

She's not the strongest swimmer,
but look at how she handles
resistance, how she frees
a corner from the skimmer

that wanted them aground,
how she won't let the breeze
that just blew out your candles
push them around.

Apparent

memory of Evan, four or five years old

If it had been an open
window you would've kept
walking, but because
it was sun-puzzled glass
you saw me through, you stopped
halfway across the yard,
and squinted through the glare,
and waved, and seemed to wait
for something else to happen,

and finally it became
apparent that it had
already, and that you
were being kept from what
you'd been about to do
by nothing, and you gave
me one more gentle wave —
I'm here, you're there —
and left me in my frame.

Street View

When I decide to let my son pursue
me like a tiger swallowtail through
Seattle, I begin in outer space,
double-click down to 16th Avenue
and take the floating arrows north until
I see his blurred-out, fascinated face.
He can't keep up with me for long — he's still
a six-year-old, and running up a hill.
But there he is, in that year's jacket, racing
the awesome camera car, and there he'll be
until it comes around again, effacing
the rest of him for all the world to see,
although, again, it's not the world he's chasing
up this street at midnight, it's just me.

Notes

ETHER MONUMENT: The italicized concluding lines are taken from an inscription on the Ether Monument in Boston's Public Garden.

TURKEYS AND STRIPPERS: Mose Wright was the elderly uncle of Emmett Till; he moved to Chicago because he could not go on safely living in Mississippi after identifying Till's killers in court. Tonton Macoute was a brutal Haitian paramilitary force employed by the dictator "Papa Doc" Duvalier.

TRANSACTION: Mt. Oread is the hill in Lawrence, Kansas, on which the University of Kansas campus sits. Red and blue are the university's colors. Massachusetts Street is named for the Massachusetts Emigrant Aid Company, an anti-slavery organization that founded Lawrence in 1854. The words "the man who gave the land / beneath it" do not refer to a specific historical figure.

STAY is an imitation of Frost's "Nothing Gold Can Stay."

THE SONG OF STATIONARY NATHAN is an imitation of Yeats's "The Song of Wandering Aengus."

SUMMER MIX: "Telephone Road" is a song by Steve Earle.

A NOTE ABOUT THE AUTHOR

Photograph: © Kelly Magerkurth, 2015

Eric McHenry is the poet laureate of Kansas. His previous collections include *Potscrubber Lullabies*, which received the Kate Tufts Discovery Award, and *Mommy Daddy Evan Sage*, a book of children's poems illustrated by Nicholas Garland. His poems have appeared in *The New Republic*, *Yale Review*, *Cincinnati Review*, *Field*, *Orion*, *The Guardian*, *Poetry Daily* and *Poetry Northwest*, from whom he received the 2010 Theodore Roethke Prize. He lives in Lawrence, Kansas, with his wife and two children and teaches creative writing at Washburn University.

Other Books from Waywiser

Other Books from Waywiser

Matthew Thorburn, *This Time Tomorrow*
Cody Walker, *Shuffle and Breakdown*
Cody Walker: *The Self-Styled No-Child*
Deborah Warren, *The Size of Happiness*
Clive Watkins, *Already the Flames*
Clive Watkins, *Jigsaw*
Richard Wilbur, *Anterooms*
Richard Wilbur, *Mayflies*
Richard Wilbur, *Collected Poems 1943-2004*
Norman Williams, *One Unblinking Eye*
Greg Williamson, *A Most Marvelous Piece of Luck*
Greg Williamson, *The Hole Story of Kirby the Sneak and Arlo the True*

FICTION

Gregory Heath, *The Entire Animal*
Mary Elizabeth Pope, *Divining Venus*
K. M. Ross, *The Blinding Walk*
Gabriel Roth, *The Unknowns**
Matthew Yorke, *Chancing It*

ILLUSTRATED

Nicholas Garland, *I wish ...*
Eric McHenry and Nicholas Garland, *Mommy Daddy Evan Sage*
Greg Williamson, *The Hole Story of Kirby the Sneak and Arlo the True*

NON-FICTION

Neil Berry, *Articles of Faith: The Story of British Intellectual Journalism*
Mark Ford, *A Driftwood Altar: Essays and Reviews*
Richard Wollheim, *Germs: A Memoir of Childhood*

* Co-published with Picador